ROLLER COASTERS

JIM BRUSH

EDGE FRANKLIN WATTS

LONDON·SYDNEY

First published in 2011 by
Franklin Watts
338 Euston Road
London NW1 3BH

Franklin Watts Australia
Level 17/207 Kent Street
Sydney NSW 2000

Series editor: Adrian Cole
Art director: Jonathan Hair
Design: Blue Paw Design
Picture research: Diana Morris
Consultants: Fiona M. Collins, Roehampton University

A CIP catalogue record for this book is available from the British Library.

ISBN: 978 1 4451 0218 4

Dewey Classification: 791'.068

Acknowledgements:
Anton Balazh/Shutterstock: endpapers. Richard Bannister/www.themeparks.ie: 3, 12, 14, 18, 22,
33. Mark Bassett/Alamy: 21. Bettmann/Corbis: 9t. Daniel Cournoyer: 40. Paul Drabek/www.
Negative-G.com: 37. Rolf Haid/epa/Corbis: 24. Jonathan Hawkins/www.jonathanhawkins.net: 34.
Scott Heckel/AP/PAI: 41t. James King-Holmes/Science Photo Library: 36. Loyce Hood Photo/PD/www.
loycehoodphoto.com: 11. Hulton Archive/istockphoto: 8. Image Bank/Getty Images: 16. © Timothy
Jones: 35. JTB Photocommunications.inc/Alamy: 32. Courtesy Kings Island./www.visitkingsisland.com:
15t. Christian Kober/Robert Harding PL/Alamy: 6. Jim Young Lee/Shutterstock: 15b. Bruce McGowan/
Alamy: 20. Brett Mulcahy/Shutterstock: front cover. Joel A. Rogers/www.coastergallery.com: 9b, 19, 25,
39t. Toby da Silva/Alamy: 23. © Snackfight: 13. www.flickr.com/photos/snackfight/456588314. So
Hung-Keung/Corbis: 7 inset. Martin Thomas/Alamy: 17. varioimages/Alamy: 39b. David Wall/Alamy: 7
main. Patrick Walters/www.coasterimage.com: 38.

Printed in China

Franklin Watts is a division of Hachette Children's Books,
an Hachette UK company.

Contents

Words that are highlighted can be found in the glossary.

What is a roller coaster?

Few of us get the chance to ride in a jet fighter or blast off in a space rocket, but we can enjoy the same 'rush' by riding on roller coasters or other extreme thrill rides.

A roller coaster is like a runaway train. A set of wheeled **cars** – called a **train** – rolls downhill on a track that rises and falls around loops and turns. Thrill rides spin, flip and fall to make you scream!

This roller coaster in Japan plunges through a pool! ❗

Go Turbo Thrills

The oldest roller coaster still in use is the Leap-the-Dips ride in Altoona, Pennsylvania, USA. Built in 1902, it has an oak track 442 metres (m) long. Its top speed is a very gentle 16 **kph**.

Find out more about loops like this on page 18.

The Ocean Park roller coaster in Hong Kong has amazing views.

Look out for these buttons to find out more about the roller coasters on page 42.

Runaway trains

The first roller coasters were the 'flying mountains' built in Russia in the 1600s. These were giant wooden ramps covered in thick ice. Riders shot down the slope on sleds and crash-landed in a sand pile.

People used wooden sleds on this flying mountain.

The first true roller coaster opened in 1884 at Coney Island near New York, USA. It was known as the Switchback Railway. In the 1900s, roller coasters got bigger and faster.

Steam power, used to pull roller coasters up the **lift hill**, was replaced by electric motors. This is the Pacific Palisades, Los Angeles, California, USA, in 1910.

GT Top Fact

The names of roller coasters often describe how they look, such as the Sooperdooperlooper (below) and the Twisted Twins. ❗

ONLINE//:

http://www.ultimaterollercoaster.com/coasters/history
Huge roller coaster website featuring a detailed timeline.

Getting going

Amusement parks build faster and more extreme roller coasters every year, but most of them work in the same way.

A roller coaster has no engine. For most of the ride, the train is moved by gravity. Gravity is the pull of the Earth on other objects. It's the force that makes an apple fall, and it stops us floating into space!

Lift hill – the roller coaster is pulled up by motors

Gravity pulls the roller coaster down

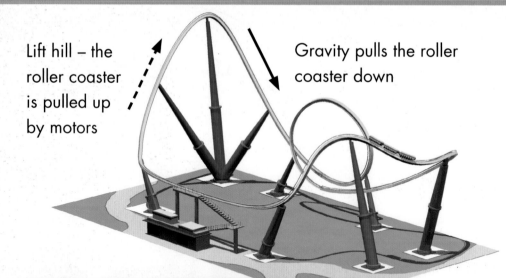

GT Top Fact

Modern rides often have a catapult system. This shoots the roller coaster off at high speed. Some catapults use very powerful magnets. Others have wheels that spin very fast.

Before gravity can get to work, the roller coaster needs to be in a high place. At the start of the ride, motors drag the train to the top of the first hill. This is often done using a long length of chain running under the track, called a **chain lift**.

The SheiKra waits four seconds before dropping through 90 degrees.

Go Turbo Thrills

The Vild-Svinet 'Wild Boar' roller coaster in Denmark has a 97 degree first drop. 90 degrees is straight down, so this ride tilts you over towards the ground.

ONLINE//:

http://www.rcdb.com/2163.htm
Webpage for the Vild-Svinet roller coaster on the Roller Coaster Database.

How roller coasters work

Once the roller coaster cars set off down the first hill, gravity takes over and pulls them along.

When the tracks slope down, the cars speed up. When they slope up, the cars slow down. This change in speed is what makes roller coasters so much fun.

Riding down a tight turn on the Silver Star **hypercoaster**. ❗

As a roller coaster train races down a hill, it picks up momentum. This is the force of an object once it gets going. At the end of the ride, the train wheels rub against the track, creating **friction**. This force slows the train down until it comes to a stop.

GT *Top Fact*

Feeling fit? The Skycycle in Okayama, Japan, is a pedal-powered roller coaster!
 What crazy ideas can you think of for a new roller coaster?

Keep pedalling! The Skycycle is at Washuzan Highland Park, Japan.

ONLINE//:

http://www.learner.org/interactives/parkphysics/ coaster.html Build your own roller coaster, then check out your fun and safety ratings.

Wooden roller coasters

Today, most roller coasters are made from steel, but there are still around 150 rides, including the famous Son of Beast (below), made from wood.

At 66 m high, Son of Beast in Mason, Ohio, USA is the tallest wooden roller coaster in the world.

If all the beams used to build it were placed end to end, they would stretch over 480 km. When it was first built in 2000, Son of Beast had the world's first wooden loop-the-loop. (It was removed in 2006.)

GT Record

The longest wooden roller coaster is still The Beast – Son of Beast's 'daddy'. This ride lasts over four minutes.

GT Top Fact

A loop-the-loop is a simple 360 degree **inversion**. A **corkscrew** is an extended loop (right) which inverts several times.

ONLINE//:

http://www.visitkingsisland.com/public/park/rides/
thrill_rides/index.cfm   Kings Island is the home of The Beast
and Son of Beast. The site includes photos and more information.

Feeling the force

People ride roller coasters because they love the feeling of gravity pulling them left, right, up or down as they speed along.

Some rides balance the forces of gravity (**g-force**) and speeding up (acceleration). This makes you feel weightless, like a skydiver falling through the air.

Go Turbo Thrills

In a sharp turn, the force on your body is up to five times as strong as gravity, known as 5Gs. Astronauts only feel 3Gs when blasting off in a rocket!

As you speed up and slow down, you are pressed into your seat or against the bar in front of you. Without this bar, you might fall out. People can experience the danger and excitement of speeding through the air, without being in any real danger.

Whizzing around makes some people scream or laugh.

GT Top Fact

Yuck! Watch out for the damp patch. On the Flying Turns ride at Cleveland, Ohio, USA extra cushions were put out to replace those that got damp from frightened riders wetting themselves.

ONLINE//:

http://www.coasterforce.com/flying_turns
Coasterforce website featuring a page on the Flying Turns bobsled coaster, which includes construction images.

Going loopy!

Most modern roller coasters loop-the-loop or corkscrew – turning the whole world upside down for a few seconds.

The force of travelling around in a loop pushes you outward and back into your seat, so it's a good job you're strapped in. Other loops include **cobra rolls** and **diving loops**.

Inverted roller coasters, such as Nemesis, also have corkscrews.

GT Record

Only two rides in the world have ten loops in one track, Colossus in Chertsey, England, and the 10 Inversion roller coaster in Guangdong, China.

Effects are also built into the track to scare passengers. Headchoppers are support bars that look like they could cut your head off. Zero-G rolls make you feel weightless.

On the Dragon Challenge roller coaster in Orlando, Florida 🛈 (shown below), two trains travel in opposite directions. They pass within 30 cm of each other three times, while travelling at speeds of 100 kph.

ONLINE//:

http://www.themeparkreview.com/coastertube/play. php?vid=10_inversion_coaster_aj4f CoasterTube – featuring videos of roller coaster rides, including one of 10 Inversion.

Crazy rides

Some thrill rides and roller coasters have taken fear to another level!

If you take the Insanity ride in Las Vegas, USA a huge arm moves your seat 20 m over the edge of the Stratosphere hotel. Then it spins you around at 64 km an hour. Then the seats swing back, forcing you to look down – all 274 m to the ground!

GT Top Fact

In a flying roller coaster, such as the Stingray in Suzhou, China, riders lie on their backs facing the sky, giving them the feeling of flying.

The Eejanaika roller coaster in Yamanashi, Japan ❗ has seats that can rotate 360 degrees backwards or forwards.

Go Turbo Thrills

The Eejanaika track also twists over five times, so all together the riders are flipped upside down 14 times during the ride – a world record.

ONLINE//:

http://www.youtube.com/watch?v=YpRFjSM_0G4
Video on YouTube of the Stratosphere Insanity thrill ride, plus links to videos of other rides and roller coasters.

To the limit

Over the last ten years, roller coasters and thrill rides have become more extreme – higher, taller, longer and faster.

In 2000, the first **gigacoaster** was built – the Millennium Force – which was 94 m high. The same year, the Steel Dragon 2000 was built in Nagashima, Japan (above). It has the longest track in the world at 2,479 m long. It was built with extra steel due to the risk from earthquakes. As a result, it cost over £32,000,000.

Most roller coasters are controlled by computers to slow them down safely. Some have special **magnetic brakes**, which are smoother than friction brakes. The X-Scream thrill ride in Las Vegas has magnetic brakes.

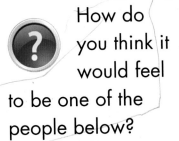

How do you think it would feel to be one of the people below?

Go Turbo Thrills

The X-Scream sits 266 m above the streets of Las Vegas, USA. It's like a giant seesaw that hangs over the edge of a building.

ONLINE//:

http://www.coasterclub.org
The European Coaster Club website. Click on 'Gallery' and '2009 Trips: South Korea and Japan' to see a photo report from Nagashima.

Building the King

The Kingda Ka ❗ is the world's tallest and fastest roller coaster. It is 139 m high and the roller coaster cars are launched at a speed of 206 kph!

The Kingda Ka is taller than a 45-storey building. It wasn't easy building such a big structure, which contains over 950 m of steel track. It took six months just to make the concrete **foundations**, which were 15 m wide for the main tower.

GT Top Fact

Cranes and platforms like these are used to build roller coasters. Some sections of the Kingda Ka track were 12 m long.

What's it like to ride the world's fastest roller coaster?

1. The Kingda Ka starts with a bang, using two huge spinning motors to fire the roller coaster up the main tower.

2. The track twists 90 degrees to the right before it reaches the top.

Go Turbo Thrills

The Kingda Ka accelerates from 0 to 206 kph in just 3.5 seconds.

3. Then the train plunges 127 m down through a 270 degree **spiral**.

4. The train climbs the second hill of 39 m, producing a moment of zero-G weightlessness, or "**air time**", before coming to a halt. Total ride time: 59 seconds.

ONLINE//:

http://www.sixflags.com/greatadventure/rides/kingdaka.aspx
The Six Flags webpage of Kingda Ka, which includes a video.

Riding the Dragon

Written by Leon Read   Illustrated by Kevin Hopgood

I feel as though I want to throw up – and we aren't
even on the roller coaster yet. I'm standing in the
morning queue with my cousins Aki and Nobu. They
are laughing and joking while sipping on an extra large
cola each. We're waiting to ride the Steel Dragon 2000.

"Hey, Ren. You know about the accident, right?" Aki says in Japanese. I hardly hear him. All my attention is on the distant screams of people already on the roller coaster.

"What accident?"

They both snigger.

"This guy, he broke his hip on this ride. Back in 2003, when a wheel came off the front car at 150 kph."

They know I've never been on a roller coaster. But this is the last day of my trip to Japan, and they are determined to get the last laugh.

I must look green or something, because they look pleased, still slurping their cola.

"This is a killer ride," Nobu says.

"Great," I sigh. My stomach twists round again.

The roller coaster seat restraint squeezes my legs, but I hardly have time to worry as we start the climb up the first hill. I know what's coming – a 94-metre dive down on the other side. And it's just the beginning of the longest roller coaster track in the world. The view up here is actually pretty cool, with Nagashima Spa Land laid out below like a toy amusement park. The Sun glints in my eyes. You can see right out to the coast. The wind is blowing too, but not hard enough to make them close the ride for the day.

The climb takes so long, and we are up so impossibly high, I almost forget about the drop when it happens. The world is pulled from under me, and I'm falling, sweeping down to Earth like a giant bird. People start screaming. Then we rise up and down again, towards the ground and round into a tight turn. My head feels like it's going to fly off!

Before I know it, I'm waving my arms in the air like the others. Screaming really loudly, from somewhere deep inside me.

"Woooooo! Hooooooo!"

The speed forces tears from my eyes. Aki and Nobu don't look so good though.

We dive down again and twist round under the supports of the roller coaster, then into the hops: eight short hills close together. Oh, this is great! I start laughing and I can't stop. We race through the two tunnels and then before I realise, the brakes come on and we slide to a stop.

Aki and Nobu climb out. Aki really looks ill. He grabs Nobu's cap from his back pocket and spews out a sickly mix of cola and hotdog. It overflows the cap and splatters out on to the platform. The guy in the booth goes mad! Ha! I grab my mobile and snap a shot – a perfect memory of my ride on the Dragon.

Tower drops

Some thrill rides make the most of our natural fear of heights. They lift a cabin, or "gondola", to the top of a tall tower – then just let go!

The Big Shot thrill ride is the highest drop tower in the world. Though the drop is around 50 m, it takes place 329 m above the ground. The gondola bounces up and down three times, like a bungee jump.

The Big Shot is on top of the Stratosphere Tower in Las Vegas.

Go Turbo Thrills

The record-breaking Giant Drop in Australia (right) is 119 m high and reaches a speed of 140.6 kph.

A winch system hoists the gondola up. Near the bottom, magnetic brakes slow the gondola down before it hits the ground. For extra thrills, some of these "scream machines" spin around. What do you think it would be like on a tower drop?

ONLINE//:

http://www.dreamworld.com.au/Rides/Thrill-Rides/The-Giant-Drop.aspx
Official Dreamworld, Gold Coast website with Giant Drop stats.

In the dark

Dark rides are built indoors or dive underground. This means part of the ride takes place in the dark, adding to the scream factor.

In the dark, you can't see hair-raising twists or falls coming. Flashing lights also add to the thrills. The Rock'n'Roller Coaster at Disney-MGM in Hollywood has a very loud soundtrack of rock music blasting the riders senses, plus a high-speed launch.

Riders prepare for the Men In Black Alien Attack dark ride at Universal Studios, Florida.

On some dark rides, passengers are armed with laser guns and shoot at targets during the ride. In others, like Expedition Everest at Walt Disney World (below), riders travel backwards in the dark.

Go Turbo Thrills

Castle of Chaos, Utah, USA, combines:
- a 3D movie shot in a real medieval castle
- a spinning platform with 25 seats
- sensors that release smoke, water and foul smells
- speakers that blast out blood-curdling screams
- **animatronic** figures that scare riders!

ONLINE//:

http://disneyworld.disney.go.com/parks/animal-kingdom/attractions/expedition-everest Webpage for the Expedition Everest roller coaster featuring photos and a video.

Super ridefilms

Ridefilms and motion platforms make you feel as if you are inside a film or a moving vehicle.

The first motion simulators were small rooms built like the cockpit in a plane or a Space Shuttle. The rooms were built on top of a machine that used computer-controlled **hydraulic** arms to lift and move it.

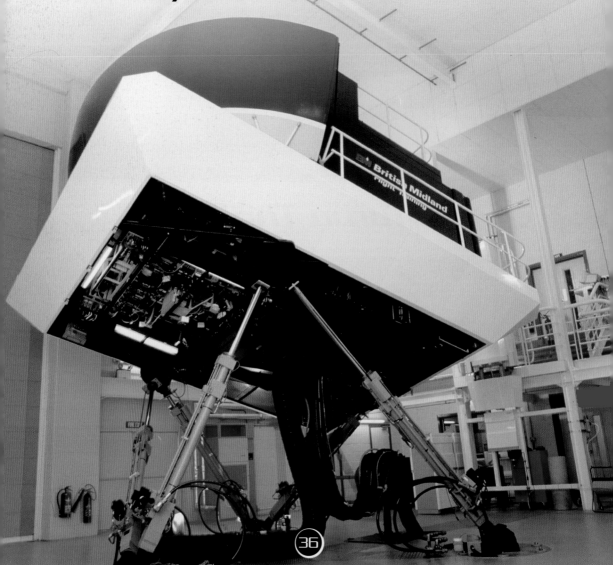

Today, motion platforms use similar technology. Passengers watch a film of a journey on a surround screen, from a flight through outer space to a ride on a roller coaster.

In a ridefilm, the seats only move a few centimetres at a time. But adding this movement to films and sounds tricks your mind into thinking you are really there.

GT Top Fact

Computers are used to design most modern roller coasters. Here the designer has created a slammer – a flat piece of track at the bottom of a long drop where riders are slammed into their seats!

ONLINE//:

http://kids.discovery.com/games/rollercoasters/
buildacoaster.html
Build your own roller coaster and get a fear rating.

Wet and wild

Amusement parks have always used water as a way to make rides more fun. Some roller coasters thunder down towards a pool of water with a big splash.

Go Turbo Thrills

The Diamondback is one of only five roller coasters to feature a **splashdown**.

The Griffon at Busch Gardens, Williamsburg, USA (above) skids over the water at the end of the ride. It also has very unusual seats. Can you see why they are more scary than most?

Be warned: many wet rides are designed to soak the passengers at some point. That said, it may be just what you need to cool off on a hot summer's day!

ONLINE//:

http://www.kidiamondback.com
Website for the Diamondback roller coaster, Kings Island, featuring videos, a photo gallery and tons of downloadables.

Coaster crash

The powerful g-forces that push and pull on a roller coaster ride can also injure passengers – and even knock them out.

Roller coaster designers work hard to make rides as safe as possible. Dummies make the first ride, but accidents do happen.

GT Top Fact

In 2001, 22 people were hurt when the brakes failed on the Superman: Ride of Steel ❶ roller coaster (above). One train crashed into another at the **loading platform**.

Rides are often rebuilt after accidents. The Rattler in San Antonio, Texas caused 100 injuries in three months, from bloody noses to back strains. As a result, its first drop was shortened by 13 m.

GT Top Fact

In July 2000, more than 20 people were hurt riding the Son of Beast. Inspectors found that the wooden train was too heavy. Lighter cars are now used.

ONLINE//:

www.gerstlauer-rides.de
Website of Gerstlauer, the builders of Son of Beast. Check out the simulators, downloads and company history.

Fast facts

Page 6: The roller coaster at Yokohama Cosmoworld, Kanagawa, Japan. The ride includes a dive through a fountain into a tunnel.

Page 9: Sooperdooperlooper at Hershey Park, Pennsylvania, USA. The ride includes a single vertical loop and was built by Schwarzkopf in 1977.

Page 9: Twisted Twins (originally called Twisted Sisters) at Six Flags Kentucky Kingdom, Louisville, USA. The tracks are named "Lola" and "Stella".

Page 11: SheiKra in Tampa Bay, Florida, USA, is a dive roller coaster, featuring a 90 degree drop to the ground, an inversion and a water blast.

Page 12: Silver Star at Europa Park, Rust, Germany, is the tallest coaster in Europe at 73 m. It was built by Bolliger & Mabillard in 2002.

Page 18: Nemesis at Alton Towers, Uttoxeter, UK, was Europe's first inverted roller coaster when it was opened in 1994.

Page 19: Dragon Challenge at the Wizarding World of Harry Potter, USA, is a pair of duelling roller coasters, opened in 2010.

Page 21: Eejanaika was designed by S&S Arrow – its name means "Ain't it great".

Page 24: Kingda Ka is at Six Flags, New Jersey, USA. It has four trains which carry 18 riders each.

Page 40: Superman: Ride of Steel at Six Flags New England, USA, was re-named Bizarro in 2009.

Answers

These are suggested answers to questions in this book. You may find in some instances that you have other answers. Talk about them with your friends. They may have other answers too.

Page 13: The answer to this is limited only by your imagination. For example you could have a rocket-powered roller coaster, or one that had a jump in the track. But there are a few things to consider. Your roller coaster should be scary, but it also needs to be safe. Where will you build it? What will you call it?

Page 23: Before the X-Scream tips over the side, you might be feeling a little nervous or really excited. But when it rolls over the edge, you'll be screaming; you might hold on tight and your heart will beat faster. That's because your brain thinks you are really going to fall!

Page 33: Have you ever been over a hump-back bridge in a car – when your stomach "gets left behind"? Well that's how it feels, only a hundred times better! Perhaps some of your friends have been on a big drop ride. How did they feel when the gondola dropped?

Page 39: Instead of a train of cars, the ride has wide rows of seats with no floors, sides or backs!

More websites

All the latest news, reviews and a glossary of different types of roller coaster:
http://www. thecoastercritic.com

Website of Hershey Park, home of the Sooperdooperlooper:
http://www.hershey park.com

Website of Cedar Point, home of Millennium Force:
http://www.cedar point.com

Website of Holiday World, home of The Voyage:
http://www.holiday world.com/rides/voyage

Home of one of the biggest roller coaster constructors featuring different types of roller coaster and photos:
http://www.bolliger-mabillard.com

Video of Dodonpa, one of the fastest roller coasters in the world:
http://www.themepark review.com/coastertube/ play.php?vid=dodonpa

Photos of the Leap-the-Dips ride in Pennsylvania:
http://www.ridezone. com/rides/coasters/ ltd99/index.htm

Website of Europa Park, home of the Silver Star, featuring a downloadable virtual ride:
http://www.europapark. de/lang-en/Park-Attractions/Attractions/ Silver-Star/c447.html

Website of Kings Dominion, home of Intimidator 305 and Dominator:
http://www. kingsdominion.com/ attractions/category. cfm?ac_id=13

Glossary

Air time – the floating feeling you get, usually felt on a drop or at the crest of a hill, while riding a roller coaster.

Animatronic – mechanical robots that are designed to look and sound like animals.

Car – one or more rows of seats for riders.

Chain lift – pulls the car or train to the top of a hill and then releases the train to roll down a hill.

Cobra roll – a double inversion. After entering a cobra roll riders are flipped upside down twice and exit heading the opposite direction to the way they came in.

Corkscrew – a twisting inversion designed like a corkscrew.

Diving loop – an inversion combining half a vertical loop and a twisting curve leading in or out of the inversion.

Foundations – the support for a structure, usually a wide base built into the ground area.

Friction – the force created when one surface rubs against another.

G-force – a unit of force used when an object is accelerated.

Gigacoaster – a roller coaster that is over 90 m tall.

Hydraulic – powered by the pressure of oil forced through pipes by a pump.

Hypercoaster – a roller coaster that is over 60 m tall.

Inversion – part of a roller coaster track that turns riders upside down.

Kph – speed measured in kilometres per hour.

Lift hill – the part of the track where the roller coaster is pulled or pushed up a hill, usually at the start of the ride.

Loading platform – where riders board roller coaster trains.

Magnetic brakes – a device that uses the force of magnets to slow or stop a roller coaster.

Spiral – a series of loops.

Splashdown – when a roller coaster drops into water. Some have scoops that send water shooting up as the train passes.

Train – two or more cars linked together.

Index